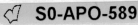

BIG BAND
SWING

MELODY LINE, CHORDS AND LYRICS
FOR KEYBOARD • GUITAR • VOCAL

HAL•LEONARD®

ISBN 0-634-02914-2

Printed in Canada

HAL•LEONARD®
CORPORATION

7777 W. BLUEMOUND RD. P.O. BOX 13819 MILWAUKEE, WI 53213

Visit Hal Leonard Online at
www.halleonard.com

(contents continued)

AMOR
(Amor, Amor, Amor)

Music by GABRIEL RUIZ
Spanish Words by RICARDO LOPEZ MENDEZ
English Words by NORMAN NEWELL

Tempo Beguine

A - mor, A - mor, A -
A - mor, *A - mor,* *A -*

mor _____ This word so
mor _____ *Na - cio de*

sweet that I re - peat Means I a -
ti, *Na - cio de mi* *de la es - pe -*

dore you. _____ A - mor, A -
ran - za. _____ *A - mor,* *A -*

mor, my love, _____ Would you de -
mor, *A - mor* _____ *Na - cio de*

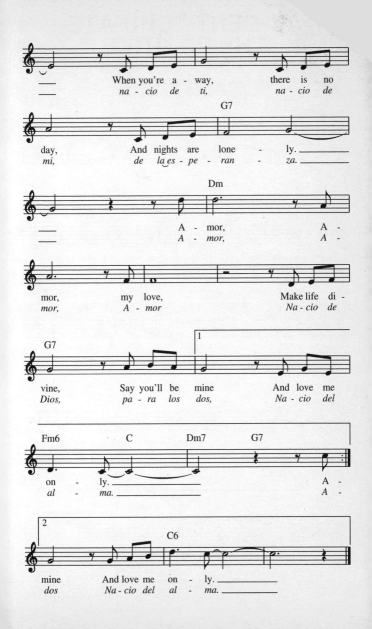

C-CENT-TCHU-ATE
THE POSITIVE

the Motion Picture HERE COME THE WAVES

Lyric by JOHNNY MERCER
Music by HAROLD ARLEN

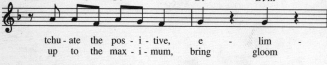

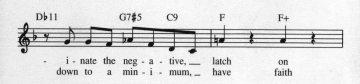

11

AIN'T MISBEHAVIN'

from AIN'T MISBEHAVIN'

Words by ANDY RAZAF
Music by THOMAS "FATS" WALLER and HARRY BROOKS

Fm7　　　Bb9　　　Eb　Ab　Eb　D7b9　G7

I'm sav-in' my love for you. ____

Cm　　　Ab7/C　　　F7/C

Like Jack Horn-er　in the cor-ner　don't go no-where,

C7　　　Bb6　Bdim7　Cm7　F9

what do I care,　Your kiss-es are worth wait-in'

Bb6　C7　F7　Bb7　Eb　Edim7

for,　be-lieve me.　I don't stay out late,

Fm7　F#dim7　Eb/G　G7#5

don't care to go.　I'm home a-bout eight, just

Ab6　Db9　Eb/G　C7

me and my ra-di-o,　ain't mis-be-hav-in'

Fm7　Bb9　Eb6

I'm sav-in' my love for you. ____

AIR MAIL SPECIAL

By BENNY GOODMAN,
JIMMY MUNDY and CHARLIE CHRISTIAN

Moderate Swing

ALRIGHT, OKAY, YOU WIN

Words and Music by SID WYCHE
and MAYME WATTS

17

Eb

all I want — from you, —

Ab9

just love — me like I love — you an' it

Eb   N.C.   Bb7

won't be hard to do! —   Well, al - right, —

Eb   Bb7   Eb   Bb+   Eb   **D.S. al Coda**

— o - kay, —   you win, —   I'm in

CODA

Ab9   Eb   Ab6 Ab9

— sweet ba - by, take me by the hand. —

Eb   Ab   Eb

— Well, al - right, —   o - kay, —

Ab Eb Ab   Eb

— you win. —

ANGEL EYES

Words by EARL BRENT
Music by MATT DENNIS

ANY PLACE I HANG MY HAT
IS HOME

from ST. LOUIS WOMAN

Words by JOHNNY MERCER
Music by HAROLD ARLEN

moves   me.

Cross ___ the riv - er,   round the   bend, _

how - dy strang - er,   so long   friend. _ There's a

voice in   the lone - some win' ___ that keeps whis - per - in'

roam!   I'm   go - in'

where a   wel - come mat is,   no   mat - ter where   that is,   'cause

an - y place I hang my hat is   home. _____

AVALON

Words by AL JOLSON and B.G. DeSYLVA
Music by VINCENT ROSE

her and Av - a - lon _____

_ from dusk _____ 'til

dawn. _____ And

so I think I'll

trav - el on _____ to

Av - a - lon. _____

_ I lon. _____

BÉSAME MUCHO
(Kiss Me Much)

Music and Spanish Words by CONSUELO VELAZQUEZ
English Words by SUNNY SKYLAR

Moderately

Bé - sa - me, _____ bé - sa - me
Bé - sa - me, _____ bé - sa - me

mu - cho; _____
mu - cho, _____

Each time I cling to your kiss I hear mu - sic di -
co - mo si fue - ra es - ta no - che la úl - ti - ma

vine; _____ bé -
vez; _____ bé -

- sa - me mu - cho, _____
- sa - me mu - cho, _____

Dm   Gsus   Gm

_____ if you should leave   me, _____
_____ bé - sa - me   mu - cho, _____

F#dim   Gm   A7

Each lit - tle dream would take   wing and   my life would be
co - mo   si   fue - ra es - ta   no - che   la   úl - ti - ma

Dm   A7   Dm   D7   Csus2/E

through; _____   bé -
vez; _____   bé -

D7   D7♭9   D+   Gsus   Gm

- sa - me   mu - cho; _____
- sa - me   mu - cho, _____

Dm

_____ Love   me   for - ev - er   and
_____ que   ten - go   mie - do   per -

E7♭9   A7   A7#5   [1] Dm

make   all   my   dreams   come   true. _____
der - te,   per - der - te   des - pués. _____

B♭9   A7sus   A7   [2] Dm   Gm6   Dm

true. _____
pués. _____

CHRISTOPHER COLUMBUS

Lyric by ANDY RAZAF
Music by LEON BERRY

Moderately

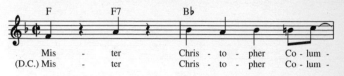

Mis - ter   Chris - to - pher   Co - lum -
(D.C.) Mis - ter   Chris - to - pher   Co - lum -

- bus __   Sailed   the
- bus, __   He   used

sea   with - out   a   com - pass; __
rhy - thm   as   a   com - pass; __

When   his
Mu - sic

men   be - gan   a   rum - pus, __
end - ed   all   the   rum - pus, __

Up   spoke
Wise   old

D9

mer - ry. _____

G7   Gm7b5   G7

Then   came   a   yell, ___   "Let's drink ___   to   Is - a -

C7   Dm9 Ab   Gm7   C7

belle,   Hum,   bring the   rum,   Ho,   Hum!"___

F   Abdim   Gm7   C7

No   more   mu - ti - ny, ___

F   Abdim   Gm7   C7

what   a   time ___   at   sea, ___

F   Abdim   Gm7   C7

with   di - plo - ma - cy, ___

F   Abdim   C7   F   **D.C. al Fine**

Chris - ty   made ___   his - to - ry. ___

THE BEST THINGS HAPPEN WHILE YOU'RE DANCING

from the Motion Picture Irving Berlin's WHITE CHRISTMAS

Words and Music by
IRVING BERLIN

BETWEEN THE DEVIL
AND THE DEEP BLUE SEA

from RHYTHMANIA

Lyric by TED KOEHLER
Music by HAROLD ARLEN

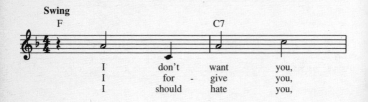

I don't want you,
I for - give you,
I should hate you,

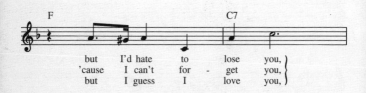

but I'd hate to lose you,
'cause I can't for - get you,
but I guess I love you,

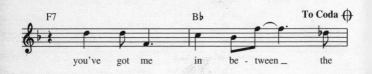

you've got me in be - tween ___ the

dev - il and the deep blue sea. ___

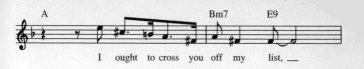

I ought to cross you off my list, ___

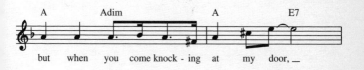

but when you come knock-ing at my door, ___

fate seems to give my heart a twist, ___ and

D.C. al Coda

I come run-ning back for more.

CODA

dev-il and the deep blue sea. ___

LUE CHAMPAGNE

Words and Music by GRADY WATTS,
FRANK RYERSON and JIMMY EATON

33

BLUE PRELUDE

Words by GORDON JENKINS
Music by JOE BISHOP

Slow Blues

Let me sigh, let me cry when I'm

blue. _____ Let me go 'way from this

lone - ly town. _____ Won't be

long till my song will be thru', _____

_ 'cause I know I'm on my last ___ go -

round. _____ All the love I could

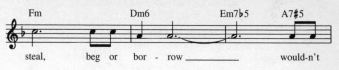

steal, beg or bor - row _____ would-n't

heal all this pain in my soul. _____

___ What is love, but a pre - lude to

sor - row _____ with a heart - break a -

head for your goal. _____ Here I go, now you

know why I'm leav - ing; _____ Got the

blues, what can I lose, __ good - bye. _____

BLUE SKIES
from BETSY

Words and Music by
IRVING BERLIN

Nev-er saw things go-ing so right. No-tic-ing the days

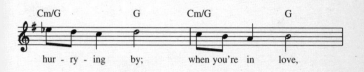

hur - ry - ing by; when you're in love,

my how they fly. Blue days, _____

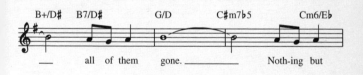

___ all of them gone. _____ Noth-ing but

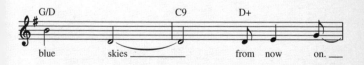

blue skies _____ from now on. ___

39

BODY AND SOUL

Words by EDWARD HEYMAN, ROBERT SOUR and FRANK EYTON
Music by JOHN GREEN

Expressively

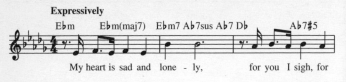

My heart is sad and lone - ly, for you I sigh, for

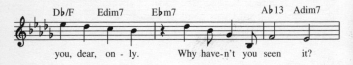

you, dear, on - ly. Why have-n't you seen it?

I'm all for you, bod-y and soul! I spend my days in

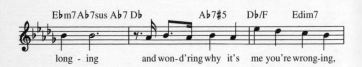

long - ing and won-d'ring why it's me you're wrong-ing,

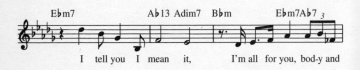

I tell you I mean it, I'm all for you, bod-y and

soul! I can't be-lieve it, it's

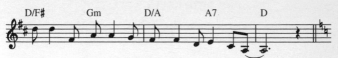

hard to con-ceive it that you'd turn a-way ro-mance.

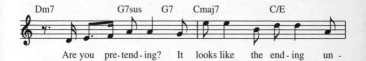

Are you pre-tend-ing? It looks like the end-ing un-

less I could have one more dance to prove, dear.

My life a wreck you're mak - ing,

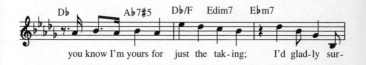

you know I'm yours for just the tak-ing; I'd glad-ly sur-

ren - der my-self to you, bod-y and

soul!   soul!

BYE BYE BLACKBIRD

from PETE KELLY'S BLUES

Lyric by MORT DIXON
Music by RAY HENDERSON

No one here can love and un - der -

stand me, oh what hard luck

sto - ries they all hand me.

Make my bed and light the light,

I'll ar - rive late to - night,

black - bird _____ bye

bye. bye. _____

CALDONIA

(What Makes Your Big Head So Hard?)

Words and Music by
FLEECIE MOORE

Medium Boogie Woogie tempo

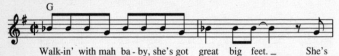

Walk-in' with mah ba-by, she's got great big feet. _ She's

long, lean and lan-ky, ain't had noth-in' to eat, but she's my

ba-by _____ and I love her just the same. _____

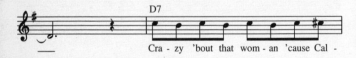

_____ Cra-zy 'bout that wom-an 'cause Cal-

don-ia is ___ her name. _____ Cal-

don-ia! Cal-don-ia! What makes your big head so

hard? But I love you, _____

CAN'T GET OUT OF THIS MOOD

from SEVEN DAYS' LEAVE

Words and Music by FRANK LOESSER
and JIMMY McHUGH

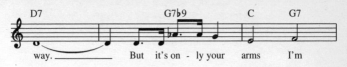

way. _____ But it's on - ly your arms I'm

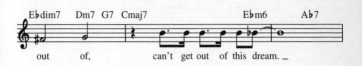

out of, can't get out of this dream. _

What a fool to dream of you; 'twas-n't part of my scheme, _

__ to sigh and tell you that I love you, but

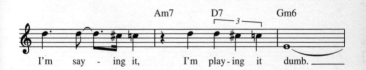

I'm say - ing it, I'm play - ing it dumb. _____

__ Can't get out of this mood; _ heart-break, here I

come! _____ here I come! _____

CARAVAN

from SOPHISTICATED LADIES

Words and Music by DUKE ELLINGTON,
IRVING MILLS and JUAN TIZOL

49

CHEROKEE
(Indian Love Song)

Words and Music by
RAY NOBLE

51

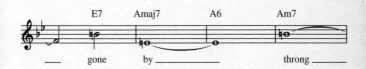

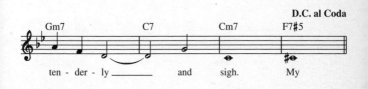

CIRIBIRIBIN

Based on the original melody by A. PESTALOZZA
English Version by HARRY JAMES
and JACK LAWRENCE

Moderate Swing

Ci – ri – bi – ri – bin,   he

waits   for   her   each   night   be -

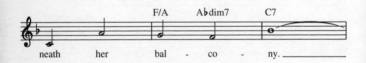

neath   her   bal – co – ny. _____

_____ Ci – ri – bi – ri – bin,   he   begs   to

hold   her   tight,   but   no,   she _____

_____ won't a – gree. _____   Ci – ri – bi – ri -

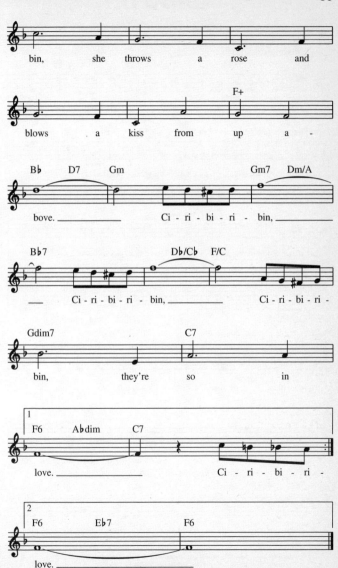

DADDY

Words and Music by
BOB TROUP

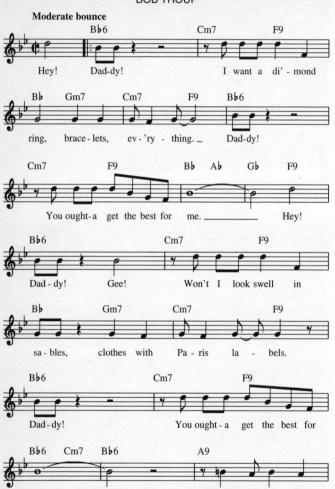

ON'T GET AROUND
MUCH ANYMORE

Words and Music by DUKE ELLINGTON
and BOB RUSSELL

Moderate Swing

Missed a Sat‑ur‑day dance,
club,

heard they crowd‑ed the floor;
got as far as the door;

could‑n't bear it with‑out ___ you, ___ }
they'd have asked me a‑bout ___ you, ___ }

don't get a‑round much an‑y‑more.

Thought I'd vis‑it the more.

Dar‑ling, I guess ___ my mind's

Cmaj7   C7   C7#5

_____ more   at   ease, _____   but

D7   F#m7b5   B7

nev - er - the - less _____

Em7   Ebdim7   D7   G7   N.C.

why stir   up mem - o - ries? __ Been   in - vit - ed   on

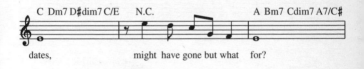

C   Dm7   D#dim7   C/E   N.C.   A   Bm7   Cdim7   A7/C#

dates,   might have gone but what   for?

N.C.   D7

Aw - f'lly   dif - f'rent with - out _____   you, __

G7   C   C/E   Ebdim7   Dm7   C

don't get   a - round much an - y - more.

C7#9

ON'T SIT UNDER
HE APPLE TREE

(With Anyone Else but Me)

Words and Music by LEW BROWN,
SAM H. STEPT and CHARLIE TOBIAS

59

DROP ME OFF IN HARLEM

Words by NICK KENNY
Music by DUKE ELLINGTON

EVERYTHING HAPPENS TO ME

Words by TOM ADAIR
Music by MATT DENNIS

Slowly

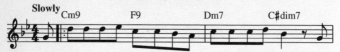

I make a date for golf and you can bet your life it rains, I
nev-er miss a thing, I've had the mea-sles and the mumps, and

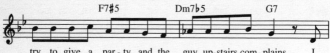

try to give a par-ty and the guy up-stairs com-plains. I
ev-'ry time I play an ace my part-ner al-ways trumps. I

guess I'll go thru life just catch-in' colds and miss-in' trains. _
guess I'm just a fool who nev-er looks be-fore he jumps. _

Ev-'ry-thing hap - pens to me. _____ I

Ev-'ry-thing hap - pens to me. _____ At

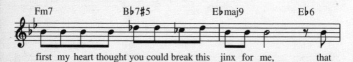

first my heart thought you could break this jinx for me, that

love would turn the trick to end de - spair. But

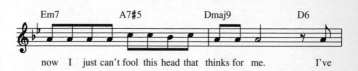

now I just can't fool this head that thinks for me. I've

mort-gaged all my cas - tles in the air. I've

tel - e-graphed and phoned, I sent an "Air-mail Spe - cial" too, your

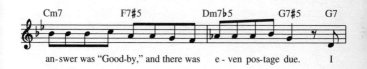

an-swer was "Good-by," and there was e - ven pos-tage due. I

fell in love just once and then it had to be with you. _

Ev - 'ry - thing hap - pens to me. ____

63

FLAT FOOT FLOOGIE

Words and Music by SLIM GAILLARD, SLAM STEWART and BUD GREEN

flou dow, __ flou dow, __ flou dow. __

If you're feel - in' low down, don't know what to do, __

__ and you want a show - down,

here's the on - ly dance for you: __ The flat foot floo-gie with the

floy floy. __ The flat foot floo - gie with the

floy floy. __ The flat foot floo - gie with the

floy floy, __ floy doy, __ floy doy, __ floy doy, __

__ floy doy. __ The __ floy doy. __

FLYING HOME

Music by BENNY GOODMAN and LIONEL HAMPTON
Lyric by SID ROBIN

Fly - ing home _ to a place that's al - ways sun - ny.

Fly - ing home _ with my pock - ets full of mon - ey.

Fly - ing home _ to my lit - tle home-town hon - ey

wait - in' for me ___ there. _____

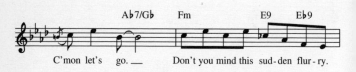

C'mon let's go. __ Don't you mind this sud - den flur - ry.

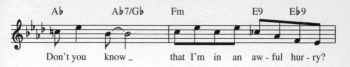

Ab   Ab7/Gb   Fm   E9   Eb9

Don't you know _ that I'm in an aw-ful hur-ry?

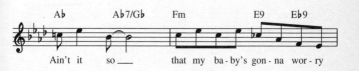

Ab   Ab7/Gb   Fm   E9   Eb9

Ain't it so ___ that my ba-by's gon-na wor-ry

Ab   Ab7

if I don't get ___ there? _____ My _

_ heart is burn - in' ev - er since I've been learn - in' how I

Db

missed {her, _____ / him, _____} since I kissed {her. _____ / him. _____} Now _

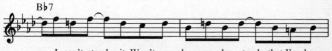

Bb7

_ I can't stand _ it. Won't you please un-der-stand _ that I've been

68

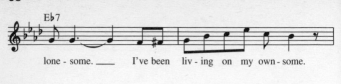

lone - some. ___ I've been liv - ing on my own - some.

Fly - ing home. _ From now on there's no more griev - in'.

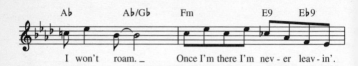

I won't roam. _ Once I'm there I'm nev - er leav - in'.

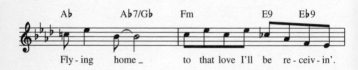

Fly - ing home _ to that love I'll be re - ceiv - in'.

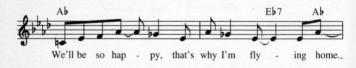

We'll be so hap - py, that's why I'm fly - ing home._

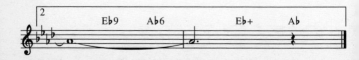

HELLO, MY LOVER, GOODBYE

Words by EDWARD HEYMAN
Music by JOHNNY GREEN

EART AND SOUL

Paramount Short Subject A SONG IS BORN

Words and FRANK LOESSER
Music by HOAGY CARMICHAEL

73

HIT THE ROAD
TO DREAMLAND

from the Paramount Picture STAR SPANGLED RHYTHM

Words by JOHNNY MERCER
Music by HAROLD ARLEN

all night ba - by

where the lit - tle Cher - ubs trod.

Look at that knocked out moon, _____ been a blow -

- in' his top ___ in the blue. ___

Nev - er saw the likes of

you; _____ What an an - gel.

I CAN'T GET STARTED WITH YOU

from ZIEGFELD FOLLIES

Words by IRA GERSHWIN
Music by VERNON DUKE

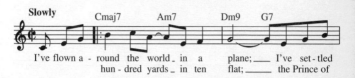

I've flown a - round the world_ in a plane;___ I've set - tled
hun - dred yards_ in ten flat;_____ the Prince of

re - vo - lu - tions in Spain; the North Pole
Wales has cop - ied my hat; with queens I've

I have chart - ed, but can't get start - ed with
a - la cart - ed, but can't get start - ed with

you. _____ A - round a
you. _____ The lead - ing

golf course I'm__ un - der par, _____ and all the
tail - ors fol - low my styles, _____ and tooth - paste

78

Bm7　E7　Bbm9　Eb9#11　D9　G9

mov - ies want _ me to star;　I've got a
ads　all fea - ture my smiles;　the As - tor -

Cmaj7　Am7　Dm9　G7b9

house, a show _ place, but I get no _ place with
bilts I vis - it, but say, what is _ it with

C9　F9　C6

you.　You're so su -
you?　When we first

Em9　Em7　A7

preme,　lyr - ics I write _ of you,
met,　how you e - lat - ed me!

Dmaj7　Gmaj9　Dmaj7

scheme　just for a sight _ of you,
Pet,　you dev - as - tat - ed me!

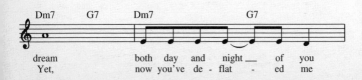

Dm7　G7　Dm7　G7

dream　both day and night _ of you
Yet,　now you've de - flat - ed me

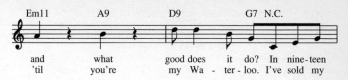

Em11   A9   D9   G7 N.C.

and   what   good does it do? In nine-teen
'til   you're   my Wa - ter - loo. I've sold my

Cmaj7   Am7   Dm9   G7

twen - ty-nine __ I sold short, _____ in Eng - land
kiss - es at __ a ba - zaar, _____ and af - ter

Bm7   E7   Bbm9 Eb9#11 D9   G9

I'm pre - sent - ed at court,   but you've got
me they've named _ a ci - gar;   but late - ly

Cmaj7   A7#5   Dm9   G9

me down-heart - ed 'cause I can't get start - ed with
how I've smart - ed, 'cause I can't get start - ed with

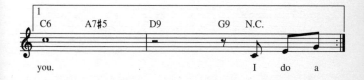

1
C6   A7#5   D9   G9 N.C.

you.   I do a

2
C6   F9   C6/9

you. _____

HOORAY FOR LOVE

from the Motion Picture CASBAH

Lyric by LEO ROBIN
Music by HAROLD ARLEN

Love! Love! Hoo - ray for love!
Some trust to fate for love.

Who is ev - er too bla - sé for love?
Oth - ers have to take off weight for love.

Make this a night for love.
Some go ber - serk for love.

If we have to fight let's fight for love.
Loaf - ers e - ven go to work for love.

Some sigh and cry for love.
Sad songs are sobbed for love.

Ah, but in Pa - ree they die for love.
Peo - ple have their nos - es bobbed for love.

I CAN DREAM, CAN'T I?

from RIGHT THIS WAY

Lyric by IRVING KAHAL
Music by SAMMY FAIN

I can see, _____ no mat-ter how

near you'll be, _____ you'll nev-er be-

long to me, but I can

dream, can't I?

Can't I pre-tend that I'm locked in the bend of

your em - brace? _____ For dreams are

just like wine, _____ and I am

I DIDN'T KNOW
WHAT TIME IT WAS
from TOO MANY GIRLS

Words by LORENZ HART
Music by RICHARD RODGERS

Moderately slow

I _____ did-n't know what time it was,

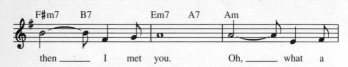

then _____ I met you. Oh, _____ what a

love-ly time it was, how sub-lime it was,

too! I _____ did-n't know what day it was.

You _____ held my hand, warm _____ like the

month of May it was, and I'll say it was grand.

I GOT IT BAD
AND THAT AIN'T GOOD

Words by PAUL FRANCIS WEBSTER
Music by DUKE ELLINGTON

Moderately

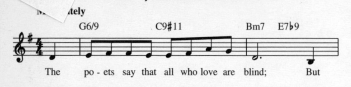

The po-ets say that all who love are blind; But

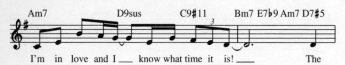

I'm in love and I ___ know what time it is! ___ The

Good Book says, "Go seek and ye shall find." Well,

I have sought and my ___ what a climb it is!

My life is just like the weath-er, it

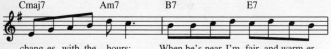

chang-es with the hours; ___ When he's near I'm fair and warm-er,

when he's gone I'm cloud-y with show-ers.

In e-mo-tion, like the o-cean, it's

ei-ther sink or swim ___ when a wom-an loves a man like

I love him.
Nev-er treats me
Like a lone-ly

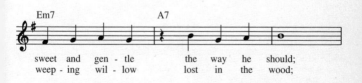

sweet and gen-tle the way he should;
weep-ing wil-low lost in the wood;

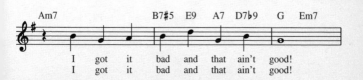

I got it bad and that ain't good!
I got it bad and that ain't good!

Am7 D7♭5 Gmaj7 Em7

My poor heart is sen - ti - men - tal
And the things I tell my pil - low

A7

not made of wood;
no wom - an should;

Am7 B7♯5 E9 A7 D7♭9

I got it bad and that ain't
I got it bad and that ain't

G Am7 B♭dim7 G/B Cmaj7

good! _____ But when the week - end's
good! _____ Tho' folks with good in -

Cm6

o - ver and Mon - day rolls a -
ten - tions tell me to save my

F7 Gmaj7 F7

roun', I end up like I
tears, I'm glad I'm mad a -

Bm7	E7	Am7

start out, just cry - in' my
bout him, I can't live with -

D7	Gmaj7

heart out. He don't love me
out him. Lord a - bove me,

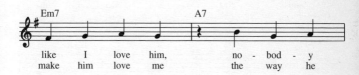

Em7	A7

like I love him, no - bod - y
make him love me the way he

Am7

could; I got it
should; I got it

B7#5	E9	A7	D7	1. G	Em7

bad and that ain't good!
bad and that ain't

Am7	D7	2. G	Cm6	G

good!

I HEAR MUSIC

from the Paramount Picture DANCING ON A DIME

Words by FRANK LOESSER
Music by BURTON LANE

I LET A SONG
GO OUT OF MY HEART

*Words and Music by DUKE ELLINGTON,
HENRY NEMO, JOHN REDMOND and IRVING MILLS*

Moderately

I let a song go out of my heart,

it was the sweet-est mel - o - dy,

I know I lost heav - en 'cause

you were the song.

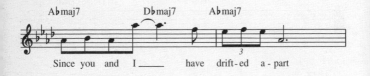

Since you and I have drift-ed a-part

I THOUGHT ABOUT YOU

Words by JOHNNY MERCER
Music by JIMMY VAN HEUSEN

I'LL BE SEEING YOU

from RIGHT THIS WAY

Lyric by IRVING KAHAL
Music by SAMMY FAIN

Freely, rubato

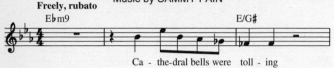

Ca - the-dral bells were toll - ing

and our hearts sang on. Was it the spell of

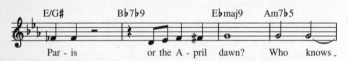

Par - is or the A - pril dawn? Who knows

if we shall meet a - gain? But when the

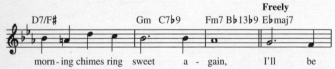

morn - ing chimes ring sweet a - gain, I'll be

see - ing you in all the old fa - mil - iar plac - es

that this heart of mine em-brac - es all day through.

Slowly, with a beat

In that small ca-fé, __ the park a-cross the way, __ the chil-dren's car-ous-el, __ the chest-nut trees, __ the wish-ing well. __ I'll be see-ing you __ in ev-'ry love-ly sum-mer's day, in ev-'ry-thing that's light and gay, I'll al-ways think of you that way. I'll find you in the morn-ing sun and when the night is new, I'll be look-ing at the moon __ but I'll be see-ing you. ____ *(Instrumental)*

I'll   be   see-ing   you __   in

ev - 'ry love - ly   sum-mer's day,   in   ev - 'ry-thing that's

light and gay,   I'll   al - ways think of   you   that way. I'll

find   you   in   the   morn - ing sun   and   when the night is

Slow

new,   I'll be look-ing at the moon, __ but I'll be see - ing

you. _____

I'M BEGINNING TO SEE THE LIGHT

Words and Music by DON GEORGE,
JOHNNY HODGES, DUKE ELLINGTON and HARRY JAMES

Moderate bounce

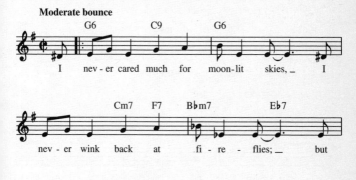

I nev-er cared much for moon-lit skies, _ I

nev-er wink back at fi-re-flies; _ but

now that the stars are in your eyes, _ I'm be-

gin-ning to see the light. ___ I

nev-er went in for af-ter-glow, _ or

Cm7　F7　B♭m7　E♭7

can - dle - light　on　the　mis - tle - toe; ___　but

G6　C9　Bm7　E7

now when you　turn　the　lamp down　low ___　I'm be -

A9　Am7　D7　G

gin - ning　to　see　the　light. ___

B9

Used　to　ram - ble　thru the　park, __

B♭9

shad - ow - box - ing　in　the　dark. __

A9

Then　you came　and　caused a　spark, _　that's a

Bbm7　　　　Eb7　　　　　Am7　　D7

four - a - larm　fi - re　now. ___　　　　　I

G6　　　　　C9　　　　　Bm7　　　　Em7

nev - er made　love　by　lan - tern　shine, _　　I

C#m7b5　　Cm7　　F7　　Bbm7　Eb7　Am7b5　D7b9

nev - er　saw　rain - bows　in　my　wine; ___　but

C#m7b5　　　C9　　　　Bm7　　　E7b5b9

now that your　lips　are　burn - ing　mine, _　I'm be -

A9　　　　Am7　　D7　　| 1 | 2
　　　　　　　　　　　　　G　Am7 D7   G

gin - ning to　see the　light. ___　　　　I　___

I'LL GET BY
(As Long As I Have You)

Lyric by ROY TURK
Music by FRED E. AHLERT

Moderately

I'll   get   by _____   as

long   as   I _____   have   you.

_____   Though   there   be   rain _____   and

dark - ness   too, _____   I'll

not   com - plain, _____   I'll

see   it   through. _____

104

I'VE GOT MY LOVE
TO KEEP ME WARM
from the 20th Century Fox Motion Picture ON THE AVENUE

Words and Music by
IRVING BERLIN

Bright Jump tempo

The snow is snow-ing, the wind is
can't re - mem - ber a worse De -

blow - ing, but I can weath - er the storm.
cem - ber; just watch those i - ci - cles form.

What do I care how
What do I care if

much it may storm?
i - ci - cles form?

I've got my love to keep me warm.

© Copyright 1936, 1937 by Irving Berlin
© Arrangement Copyright 1948 by Irving Berlin
Copyright Renewed
International Copyright Secured   All Rights Reserved

I'VE HEARD THAT SONG BEFORE

from the Motion Picture YOUTH ON PARADE

Lyric by SAMMY CAHN
Music by JULE STYNE

IF YOU CAN'T SING IT

(You'll Have to Swing It)

from the Paramount Picture RHYTHM ON THE RANGE

Words and Music by
SAM COSLOW

IN THE MOOD

By JOE GARLAND

112

IT COULD
HAPPEN TO YOU

from the Paramount Picture AND THE ANGELS SING

Words by JOHNNY BURKE
Music by JAMES VAN HEUSEN

IT'S EASY TO REMEMBER

from the Paramount Picture MISSISSIPPI

Words by LORENZ HART
Music by RICHARD RODGERS

fin - gers press me tight. _____ I'd rath - er

dream _____ than have that lone - ly feel - ing

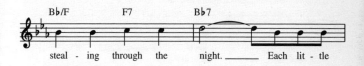

steal - ing through the night. _____ Each lit - tle

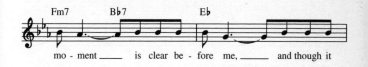

mo - ment _____ is clear be - fore me, _____ and though it

brings me re - gret, it's

eas - y to re - mem - ber, and

so hard to for - get.

JAVA JIVE

Words and Music by MILTON DRAKE
and BEN OAKLAND

(1.,3.) I love cof-fee, I love tea, __
(2..,4.) I love ja-va, sweet and hot, __

I love the Ja-va Jive and it loves me. __
whoops! Mis-ter Mo-to, I'm a cof-fee pot. __

Cof-fee and tea __ and the jiv-in' and me, __ a
Shoot me a pot __ and I'll pour me a shot, __ a

cup, a cup, a cup, a cup, a cup!
cup, a cup, a cup, a cup, a cup! Oh,

slip me a slug __ from that won-der-ful mug, __ and

I'll cut a rug __ till I'm snug __ in the jug. { A Drop

slice of on-ion and a raw one, __ draw one. __ }
me a nick-el in my pot, Joe, __ tak-in' it slow. __ }

JERSEY BOUNCE

Words by ROBERT WRIGHT
Music by BOBBY PLATTER, TINY BRADSHAW,
ED JOHNSON and ROBERT WRIGHT

Moderately

They call it that Jer - sey Bounce, _____ a

rhy - thm that real - ly counts. _____ The

tem - per - 'ture al - ways mounts _____ wher -

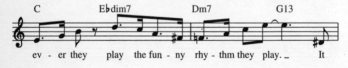

ev - er they play the fun - ny rhy - thm they play. _ It

start - ed on Jour - nal Square, _____ and

some - bod - y heard it there. _____ He

put it right on the air _____ and

JUKE BOX
SATURDAY NIGHT

from STARS ON ICE

Words by AL STILLMAN
Music by PAUL McGRANE

MP, JIVE AN' WAIL

Words and Music by
LOUIS PRIMA

Moderately fast Swing

Ba - by, ba - by, it looks like it's _ gon-na hail.
Pa-pa's in the ice-box look-ing for a _ can of ale.

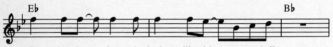

Ba - by, ba - by, it looks like it's _ gon-na hail.
Pa-pa's in the ice-box look-ing for a _ can of ale.

You bet - ter come in - side _ and let me
Ma - ma's in the back yard

teach you how to jive an' wail. _
learn - ing how to jive an' wail. _

Oh, _ you got - ta jump, jive, and

then you wail. You got - ta jump, jive, and

B

jump, jive, and then you wail. You got - ta

F#7   E7

jump, jive, and then you wail a - way.

B   B

___ You got - ta jump, jive and

then you wail. You got - ta jump, jive, and

E7

then you wail. You got - ta jump, jive, and

B

then you wail. You got - ta jump, jive, and

F#7/C#

then you wail. You got - ta jump, jive, and

Repeat and Fade

E7/F#   B G#13 Dm7   G13

then you wail a - way. _   Oh, _ you got - ta

LAZY RIVER
from THE BEST YEARS OF OUR LIVES

Words and Music by HOAGY CARMICHAEL
and SIDNEY ARODIN

Moderately

Up a la - zy riv - er by the old mill - run, that

la - zy, la - zy riv - er in the noon - day sun,

Lin - ger in the shade of a kind old tree;

throw a - way your trou - bles, dream a dream with me. __

Up a la - zy riv - er where the rob - in's song a -

wakes a bright new morn - ing, we can

loaf a - long. Blue skies up a - bove,

ev - 'ry-one's in love, up a la - zy riv - er, how

hap - py you can be, up a la - zy riv - er with

me. me.

LEAN BABY

Lyric by ROY ALFRED
Music by BILLY MAY

Moderate Swing

My lean ba - by { tall ___ / small ___

___ { and thin, ___ five feet sev - en of

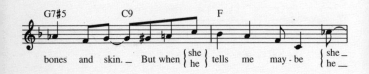

bones and skin. ___ But when { she / he } tells me may - be { she ___ / he ___

___ { loves me, ___ I feel as { mel - low as a fel - low can be. / whirl - y as a girl - y can be. ___

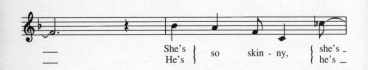

___ { She's / He's } so skin - ny, { she's ___ / he's ___

—} so drawn; — when {she he} stands side-ways you

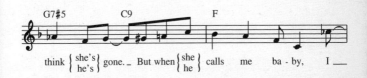

think {she's he's} gone. — But when {she he} calls me ba - by, I —

— feel fine — to think{she's he's} fran-tic - 'lly, ro-man-tic - 'lly mine..

{She's He's} slen - der —— but {she's he's}

Male alternate: I chased her —— and I

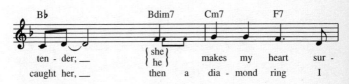

ten - der; — {she he} makes my heart sur -

caught her, — then a dia - mond ring I

ren - der. — And ev -'ry night — when

bought her. — The dia-monds shine, — the

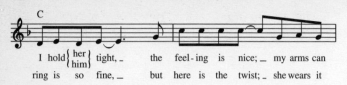

C

I hold { her / him } tight, _ the feel-ing is nice; _ my arms can

ring is so fine, _ but here is the twist; _ she wears it

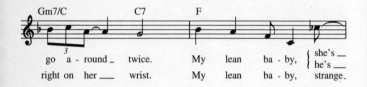

Gm7/C   C7   F

go a - round _ twice.   My lean ba - by,   { she's _ / he's _ }

right on her ___ wrist.   My lean ba - by,   strange _

Bb   Bdim7   F/C   Dm7

___ } so slim. _   A broom - stick's wid - er   { but / com - }

___ to see, _   but all that noth - ing be -

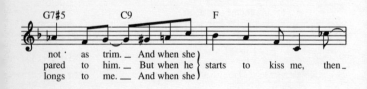

G7#5   C9   F

not ' as trim. _ And when she

pared to him. _ But when he } starts to kiss me, then _

longs to me. _ And when she }

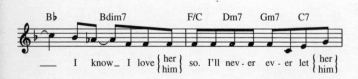

Bb   Bdim7   F/C   Dm7   Gm7   C7

___ I know _ I love { her / him } so. I'll nev - er ev - er let { her / him }

| 1 | | 2 |
| F   Db9   Gm7/C   C7 | | F   Gb9   F6/9 |

go.   go.

MANHATTAN

from the Broadway Musical THE GARRICK GAIETIES

Words by LORENZ HART
Music by RICHARD RODGERS

Dm7　　　　　　　　　　　G7

_____ the sub - way charms us so, _____
_____ your bath - ing suit so thin _____

C7

_____ when balm - y breez - es blow
_____ will make the shell - fish grin

C7♭9　　　F　　　　D7

to and fro, and tell me what street
fin to fin. I'd like to take a

Gm7　　　　C7　　　F　　　B♭6

com-pares with Mott Street in Ju - ly, _____
sail on Ja - mai - ca Bay with you; _____

Am7　　　A♭dim7　　C7/G　　　F♯dim7

_____ sweet push carts gen - tly glid -
_____ and fair Can - ar - sie's Lakes _____

C7/G　　　　C7　　C7/B♭　　Am7♭5

- ing by. _____
_____ we'll view. _____

The great big cit - y's a won - d'rous
The cit - y's bus - tle can - not de -

toy just made for a girl and
stroy the dreams of a girl and

boy.
boy.
We'll turn Man-hat - tan

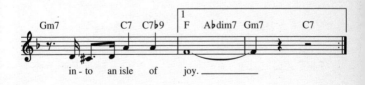

in - to an isle of joy. _____

joy. _____

LET'S DANCE

Words by FANNY BALDRIDGE
Music by GREGORY STONE and JOSEPH BONINE

135

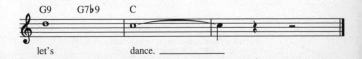

LET'S GET AWAY FROM IT ALL

Words and Music by TOM ADAIR
and MATT DENNIS

Moderate bounce

Let's take a boat _ to Ber - mu - da, _
Let's take a trip _ in a trail - er, _

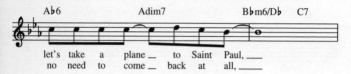

let's take a plane _ to Saint Paul, _
no need to come _ back at all, _

let's take a kay - ak to Quin - cy or Ny - ack,
let's take a pow - der to Bos - ton for chow - der,

let's get a - way _ from it all. _

let's get a - way _ from it all. _ We'll

trav - el 'round from town to town, _ we'll

Fm7 Bb7 Eb6

vis - it ev - 'ry state. A -

Bb Bdim Cm7 F9

las - ka and Ha - wa - ii, too __

Bb7 Bb7 Bb7#5

then all the fort - y - eight. __

Eb Bb7b9 Eb6 Eb7

Let's go a - gain __ to Ni - a - g'ra, __

Ab6 Adim Bbm6 C7

this time we'll look __ at the "Fall". __

Fm Bb7 Db9 C7#5 C7

Let's leave our hut, __ dear, get out of our rut, __ dear,

Fm6 E9 Eb6

let's get a - way __ from it all. __

LULLABY OF THE LEAVES

Words by JOE YOUNG
Music by BERNICE PETKERE

THE MAN WITH THE HORN

Lyric by EDDIE DE LANGE
Music by JACK JENNEY,
BONNIE LAKE and EDDIE DE LANGE

MEMORIES OF YOU
from THE BENNY GOODMAN STORY

Lyric by ANDY RAZAF
Music by EUBIE BLAKE

MOOD INDIGO
from SOPHISTICATED LADIES

Words and Music by DUKE ELLINGTON,
IRVING MILLS and ALBANY BIGARD

MOONGLOW

Words and Music by WILL HUDSON,
EDDIE DE LANGE and IRVING MILLS

Smoothly

It must have been Moon - glow,

way up in the blue,

it must have been Moon - glow

that led me straight to you; ___

I still hear you say - ing,

"Dear one, hold me fast."

And I start in pray - ing,

MOONLIGHT IN VERMONT

Words and Music by JOHN BLACKBURN
and KARL SUESSDORF

Pen - nies in a stream, fall - ing leaves, a

syc - a - more, moon - light in Ver -

mont. Ic - y fin - ger - waves,

ski trails on a moun - tain - side,

snow - light in Ver - mont.

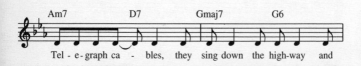

Tel - e - graph ca - bles, they sing down the high - way and

trav - el each bend __ in the road,

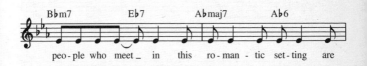

peo - ple who meet __ in this ro - man - tic set - ting are

so hyp - no - tized __ by the love - ly

eve - ning sum - mer breeze,

war - bling of a mead - ow - lark,

moon - light in Ver - mont.

You and I and moon - light in Ver - mont.

(There Ought to Be A)
MOONLIGHT SAVING TIME

Words and Music by IRVING KAHAL
and HARRY RICHMAN

There ought to be a Moon-light Sav-ing Time, _ so
I could love that girl of mine _ un-
til the bird-ies wake and chime, "Good morn-ing."
There ought to be a law in
clo-ver time _ to keep that moon out
o-ver-time, _ to keep each lov-er's
lane in rhyme _ till dawn-ing.

You'd bet - ter hur - ry up, hur - ry up,

hur - ry up, get bus - y to - day. You'd bet - ter

croon a tune, croon a tune to the man up in the moon,

and here's _ what I'd say: _____ There

ought to be a Moon - light Sav - ing Time, _ so

I could love that girl of mine _ un -

til the bird - ies wake and chime, _ "Good

morn - ing." There ing."

THE MUSIC GOES 'ROUND AND AROUND

Words by RED HODGSON
Music by EDWARD FARLEY and MICHAEL RILEY

push the mid - dle valve down; ___ the

mu - sic goes down, a - round, ___ be - low, ___ be - low, ___

___ be - low. ___ Dee-dle-dee ho - ho - ho,

list - en to the ja - azz come out. I

push the oth - er valve down; the

mu - sic goes 'round and a - round, whoa - ho -

ho - ho - ho - ho, and it comes out

here. I here.

MY SILENT LOVE

Words by EDWARD HEYMAN
Music by DANA SUESSE

I _____ reach for you like I'd reach for a
star, wor - ship - ing you from a -
far, liv - ing with my si - lent
love. I'm _____ like a
flame dy - ing out in the rain,
on - ly the ash - es re - main,
smould - 'ring like my si - lent love.

NEVERTHELESS
(I'm in Love with You)

Words and Music by BERT KALMAR
and HARRY RUBY

May - be I'm right _ and may - be I'm wrong, _ and
may - be I'm weak _ and may - be I'm strong; _ but
nev - er - the - less, ____ I'm in
love with you.
May - be I'll win _ and may - be I'll lose, _ and
may - be I'm in ____ for cry - in' the blues; _ but
nev - er - the - less, _ I'm in love with you. ____

A NIGHTINGALE SANG IN BERKELEY SQUARE

Lyric by ERIC MASCHWITZ
Music by MANNING SHERWIN

That cer-tain night, the night we met, there was
strange it was, how sweet and strange, there was

mag-ic a-broad in the air. There were
nev-er a dream to com-pare with that

an-gels din-ing at the Ritz, and a
ha-zy, cra-zy night we met, when a

night-in-gale sang in Ber-k'ley
night-in-gale sang in Ber-k'ley

Square. I
Square. This

may be right, I may be wrong, but I'm
heart of mine beats loud and fast, like a

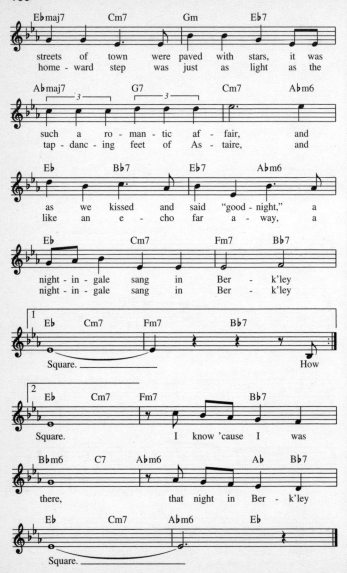

streets of town were paved with stars, it was
home - ward step was just as light as the

such a ro - man - tic af - fair, and
tap - danc - ing feet of As - taire, and

as we kissed and said "good - night," a
like an e - cho far a - way, a

night - in - gale sang in Ber - k'ley
night - in - gale sang in Ber - k'ley

Square. _____ How

Square. I know 'cause I was

there, that night in Ber - k'ley

Square. _____

ROUTE 66

By BOBBY TROUP

If you _____ ev-er plan to mo-tor west,_ _____ Trav-el my way, take the high-way that's the best. _____ Get your kicks on Route _____ Six-ty-six! _____ It winds _____ from Chi-ca-go to L. A., _____ more than two _____ thou-sand miles all the way.

F6   Gm7

_   Get your   kicks   on

C9   F   Ab dim7

Route _   Six -   ty - six! ____

Gm7   C7   F7

Now you   go   thru Saint Loo - ey   and

Bb9   F

Jop - lin, Mis-sour - i   and   Ok - la-hom - a   Cit - y   is might-

F9   Bb9

-   y   pret - ty. You'll see ____   Am-ar -

              F7   ⌐— 3 —⌐

il - lo; ____   Gal - up,   New

              Gm   C9

Mex - i - co; ____   Flag-staff, Ar - i - zon - a;

don't for - get Wi - no - na, King-man, Bar-stow,

San Ber - nar - din - o. Won't you _____ get hip

to this time - ly tip: _____

when you _____ make that

Cal - i - for - nia trip, _____

get your kicks on

Route _ Six - ty - six! _____

OLD DEVIL MOON
from FINIAN'S RAINBOW

Words by E.Y. HARBURG
Music by BURTON LANE

I look at you and sud- den- ly,
You've got me fly- in' high and wide

some- thing in your eyes I see
on a mag- ic car- pet ride

soon be- gins be- witch- ing me. _____
full of but- ter- flies in- side. _____

_____ It's that old dev- il moon _____ that you
_____ Wan- na cry, wan- na croon, _____ wan- na

stole from the skies. _____ It's that old dev- il moon _____
laugh like a loon. _____ It's that old dev- il moon _____

ON A SLOW BOAT TO CHINA

By FRANK LOESSER

Slowly

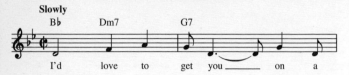

I'd love to get you _____ on a

slow boat to Chi - na, _____

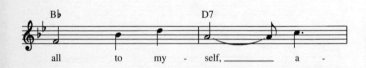

all to my - self, _____ a -

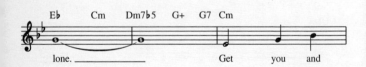

lone. _____ Get you and

keep you _____ in my arms ev - er - more, _____

_____ leave all your lov - ers _____

weep - ing on the far - a - way shore. ___

Out on the brin - y ___ with a

moon big and shin - y, ___ melt - ing your

heart ___ of stone. ___ I'd love to

get you ___ on a slow boat to Chi - na, ___

all to my - self a - lone. ___

OPUS ONE

Words and Music by
SY OLIVER

Moderate Jump tempo

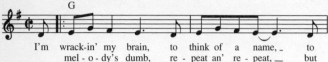

I'm wrack-in' my brain, to think of a name, to
mel - o - dy's dumb, re - peat an' re - peat, but

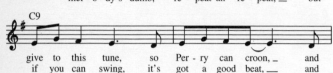

give to this tune, so Per - ry can croon, and
if you can swing, it's got a good beat, and

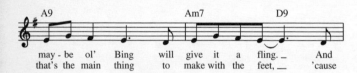

may - be ol' Bing will give it a fling. And
that's the main thing to make with the feet, 'cause

1
that - 'll start ev - 'ry - one hum - min' the thing. The

2
ev - 'ry - one is swing - in' to - day. So, I'll call it

O - pus One! It's not for Sam - my Kaye,

Bb6 — G7#5 — C9 — F9#5

_ Hey! _ Hey! _ Hey! _ It's

Db — Bbm7 — Ebm7 — Ab7b9

O - pus One! It's got to swing, not sway..

Db6 — Db13 — D13

May - be, _____ if

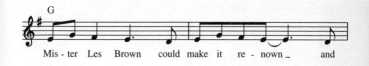

G

Mis - ter Les Brown could make it re - nown _ and

C9

Ray An - tho - ny could swing it for me, ___ there's

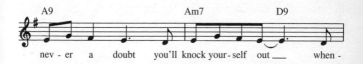

A9 — Am7 — D9

nev - er a doubt you'll knock your - self out _ when -

G — C9 — G Eb9 G

ev - er you can hear O - pus One. _____

PENTHOUSE SERENADE

Words and Music by WILL JASON
and VAL BURTON

POLKA DOTS AND MOONBEAMS

Words by JOHNNY BURKE
Music by JIMMY VAN HEUSEN

Slowly, with expression

A coun-try dance was be-ing held in a gar-den,

I felt a bump and heard an, "Oh, beg your par-don."

Sud-den-ly I saw pol-ka dots and moon-beams

all a-round a pug-nosed dream. __

The mu-sic start-ed and was I the per-plexed one,

I held my breath and said, "May I have the next one?"

In my fright-ened arms pol-ka dots and moon-beams

PRELUDE TO A KISS

Words by IRVING GORDON and IRVING MILLS
Music by DUKE ELLINGTON

SATIN DOLL

from SOPHISTICATED LADIES

Words by JOHNNY MERCER and BILLY STRAYHORN
Music by DUKE ELLINGTON

Smoothly

Cig - a - rette hold - er which wigs me,
Ba - by shall we __ go out skip - pin',

o - ver her shoul - der, she digs me.
care - ful a - mi - go, you're flip - pin'.

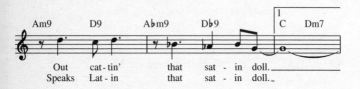

Out cat - tin' that sat - in doll. ___
Speaks Lat - in that sat - in doll. _

__ __ She's

no - bod - y's fool, so I'm play - ing it cool as can be. _

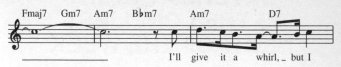

I'll give it a whirl, _ but I

ain't for no girl __ catch-ing me. ___

__ Switch E - Roo- ney. Tel - e-phone num - bers

well you know, do - ing my rhum - bas

with u - no, and that 'n'

my sat - in doll. ___

SATURDAY NIGHT IS THE LONELIEST NIGHT OF THE WEEK

Words by SAMMY CAHN
Music by JULE STYNE

SEEMS LIKE OLD TIMES

from ARTHUR GODFREY AND HIS FRIENDS

Lyric and Music by JOHN JACOB LOEB
and CARMEN LOMBARDO

Moderately

Seems like old times,
old times,

hav - ing you to walk with, seems like
din - ner dates and flow - ers, just like

old times, hav - ing you to
old times, stay - ing up for

talk with. And it's still a
hours. __ Mak - ing dreams come

thrill   just   to   have   my   arms   a -
true,   do - ing things   we   used   to

round you,   still   the   thrill   that it

was   the   day   I   found   you.   Seems like

do,   seems   like   old   times, _____

_____ be - ing here   with   you. _____

TIMENTAL JOURNEY

Words and Music by BUD GREEN, LES BROWN and BEN HOMER

Slowly

Gon - na take   a   sen - ti-men - tal jour-ney,
Got   my bag,   I   got   my res - er - va-tion,

gon - na set   my   heart   at ease. __
spent   each dime   I   could   af - ford. __

Gon - na make   a   sen - ti - tal jour-ney
Like   a   child   in   wild   an - ti - ci - pa-tion,

to   re - new old   mem - o - ries. __
long   to hear that   "All __ a - board." __

Sev - en, ____   that's   the time   we leave at

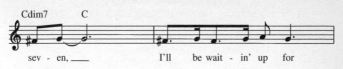

Cdim7   C

sev - en, _____   I'll   be   wait - in'   up   for

C#7   D7   D9

Heav - en, _____   count - in'   ev - 'ry   mile   of

G7   Dm7   G6   Gdim7   G9

rail - road   track __   that   takes   me   back. __

C

Nev - er thought   my   heart   could be   so "yearn-y,"

Em   Ab9   G7

why   did   I   de - cide   to   roam? _

C   F9

Got - ta   take   this   sen - ti-men - tal jour-ney,

C   G7   C

sen - ti - men - tal   jour - ney   home. _

SMALL FRY

from the Paramount Motion Picture SING, YOU SINNERS

Words by FRANK LOESSER
Music by HOAGY CARMICHAEL

Moderate Swing

Small fry, strut-tin' by the pool room,

small fry, should be in the school-room.

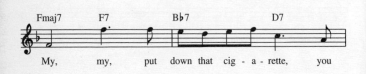

My, my, put down that cig-a-rette, you

ain't a grown-up high and might-y yet.

Small fry, danc-in' for a pen-ny,

small fry, count-in' up how man-y.

My, my, just lis-ten here to me, you

ain't the big-gest cat-fish in the sea. _____ You prac-tice

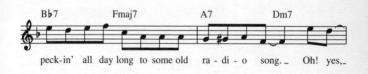

peck-in' all day long to some old ra-di-o song. _ Oh! yes,_

_ Oh! yes, _ oh yes. _____ You bet-ter

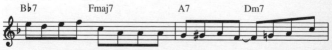

lis-ten to your Maw and some-day prac-tice the law _ and then you'll

be a real suc - cess. Yes,

small fry, you kissed the neigh-bor's daugh - ter,

small fry, should stay in shal - low wa - ter.

Seems I should take you 'cross my knee, you

ain't the big - gest cat-fish in the sea.____ You've got your

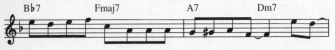

feet all soak-in' wet, you'll be the death of me yet.__ Oh! me,__

__ oh my, __ small fry.

SMOKE RINGS

Words by NED WASHINGTON
Music by H. EUGENE GIFFORD

SNOWFALL

Lyrics by RUTH THORNHILL
Music by CLAUDE THORNHILL

mist - y white,

vel - vet breeze

'round my door - step.

Gen - tly, _____

soft - ly, _____

si - lent _____ snow - fall! _____

SOLITUDE

**Words and Music by DUKE ELLINGTON,
EDDIE DE LANGE and IRVING MILLS**

SOUTH OF THE BORDER

(Down Mexico Way)

Words and Music by JIMMY KENNEDY
and MICHAEL CARR

Then she sighed as she whis-pered Ma -

Fm7   Bb7

ña - na, nev-er dream - ing that we were

Eb   C7

part - ing. And I lied as I whis-pered Ma -

Fm7   Eb Bb9

ña - na, ____ for our to - mor - row nev - er

Eb

came. South of the bor - der _____

Fm7 Bb7   Eb

____ I rode back one day; _____

there in a veil of white by

Eb/G Gbdim7 Bb7

can - dle - light she knelt to pray. _____

mist - y white,

vel - vet breeze

'round my door - step.

Gen - tly, _____

soft - ly, _____

si - lent _____ snow - fall! _____

SOLITUDE

**Words and Music by DUKE ELLINGTON,
EDDIE DE LANGE and IRVING MILLS**

In my sol - i - tude _____ you
sol - i - tude _____ you
sol - i - tude _____ I'm

haunt me with re - ver - ies _____
taunt me with mem - o - ries _____
pray - ing, dear Lord a - bove _____

_____ of days gone by. _____ In my
_____ that nev - er
_____ send back my

die. _____ I sit in my chair, I'm

filled with de - spair, there's no one could be so sad. _____ With

gloom ev - 'ry-where, I sit and I stare, I know that I'll soon go

mad. In my love. _____

The mis - sion bells told me ___

that I must - n't stay ___

south of the bor - der ___

down Mex - i - co way. ___

Ay! Ay! Ay! Ay! ___

Ay! Ay! Ay! Ay! ___

Ay! Ay! Ay! Ay! ___

Ay! Ay! Ay! Ay! ___

SOPHISTICATED LADY

from SOPHISTICATED LADIES

*Words and Music by DUKE ELLINGTON,
IRVING MILLS and MITCHELL PARISH*

They say_____ in-to your ear-ly life ro-mance came,_____ and in this heart of yours burned a flame,_____ a flame that flick-ered one day and died a - way. Then,_____ with dis-il-lu - sion deep in your eyes,_____ you learned that fools in love soon grow wise. _____ The years have changed you, some-how; I see you now.

Smok - ing, drink - ing, nev - er think - ing of to -

mor - row, non - cha - lant.

Dia - monds shin - ing, danc - ing, din - ing with some

man in a res - tau - rant, is that all you real - ly want?

No, _____ so - phis - ti - cat - ed la - dy, I

know, _____ you miss the love you lost long a -

go, _____ and when no - bod - y is nigh you

cry. _____ They cry. _____

STAR DUST

Words by MITCHELL PARISH
Music by HOAGY CARMICHAEL

And now the pur-ple dusk of twi-light time
steals a-cross the mead-ows of my heart.
High up in the sky the lit-tle stars climb,
al-ways re-mind-ing me that we're a-part.
You wan-dered down the lane and far a-way,
leav-ing me a song that will not die.
Love is now the star dust of yes-ter-day,

STEPPIN' OUT
WITH MY BABY

from the Motion Picture Irving Berlin's EASTER PARADE

Words and Music by
IRVING BERLIN

Medium Jump tempo

If I seem to scin-til-late _ it's be-cause I've

got a date, _ a date with a

pack-age of _ the good things that

come with love. _ You don't have to ask me, _

I won't waste your time. But if you should

ask me _ why I feel sub-lime, I'm _

| Dm | Dm/C | Gm/B♭ | A7 |

step - pin' out ___ with my ba - by.

| Dm | Dm/C | Gm/B♭ | A7 | Dm | Dm/C |

Can't go wrong _ 'cause I'm in right. _ It's for sure, _

| Gm/B♭ | Em7♭5 | Dm | Dm/F Gm6 |

not for may - be, that I'm all dressed

| G♯dim7 A7 Dm6 | Dm | Dm/C Gm/B♭ | A7 |

up to - night. _ Step-pin' out _ with my hon - ey,

| Dm | Dm/C | Gm/B♭ | A7 |

can't be bad ___ to feel so good. _

| Dm | Dm/C | Gm/B♭ | Em7♭5 |

Nev - er felt ___ quite so sun - ny.

| Dm | Dm/F Gm6 | G♯dim7 A7 Dm6 |

And I keep on knock - in' wood, _ there'll be

STELLA BY STARLIGHT

from the Paramount Picture THE UNINVITED

Words by NED WASHINGTON
Music by VICTOR YOUNG

The song _____ a rob - in sings _____ through years _____ of end - less springs; _____ the mur - mur of a brook at e - ven - tide _____ that rip - ples by a nook where two

STOMPIN' AT THE SAVOY

Words and Music by BENNY GOODMAN, EDGAR SAMPSON,
CHICK WEBB and ANDY RAZAF

STORMY WEATHER
(Keeps Rainin' All the Time)
from COTTON CLUB PARADE OF 1933

Lyric by TED KOEHLER
Music by HAROLD ARLEN

A STRING OF PEARLS

from THE GLENN MILLER STORY

Words by EDDIE DE LANGE
Music by JERRY GRAY

SUNRISE SERENADE

Lyric by JACK LAWRENCE
Music by FRANKIE CARLE

Good morn-in', good morn-in' you sleep-y head,— it's

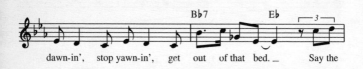

dawn-in', stop yawn-in', get out of that bed. — Say the

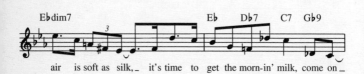

air is soft as silk,— it's time to get the morn-in' milk, come on —

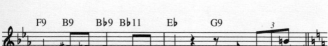

— wake up!— Get up! — Look at the grass —

_____ of that new-mown hay ___ and the sug - ar cane; _

_____ looks like to - night ___

___ there should be a moon ___ down in lov - er's lane. _

_____ There you go day - dream-ing when it's

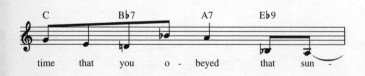

time that you o - beyed that sun -

- rise ser - e - nade. ___ Good ___

TAKE THE "A" TRAIN

Words and Music by
BILLY STRAYHORN

SWEET SUE-JUST YOU
from RHYTHM PARADE

Words by WILL J. HARRIS
Music by VICTOR YOUNG

'TAIN'T WHAT YOU DO
(It's the Way That Cha Do It)

Words and Music by SY OLIVER
and JAMES YOUNG

T OLD BLACK MAGIC

Paramount Picture STAR SPANGLED RHYTHM

Words by JOHNNY MERCER
Music by HAROLD ARLEN

That old black mag - ic has me in its spell. That old black mag - ic that you weave so well. Those i - cy fin - gers up and down my spine. The same old witch - craft when your eyes meet mine. The same old tin - gle that I

224

THERE ARE SUCH THINGS

Words and Music by STANLEY ADAMS,
ABEL BAER and GEORGE W. MEYER

THERE! I'VE SAID IT AGAIN

Words and Music by DAVE MANN
and REDD EVANS

Slowly, with expression

THERE'LL BE SOME CHANGES MADE

from ALL THAT JAZZ

Words by BILLY HIGGINS
Music by W. BENTON OVERSTREET

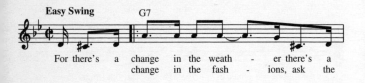

For there's a change in the weath - er there's a
change in the fash - ions, ask the

change in the sea, ___ so from now on there'll be a
fem - i - nine folks, _ e - ven Jack Ben - ny has been

change in me. ___ My walk will be dif - f'rent, my
chang-ing jokes. _ I must make some chang - es from

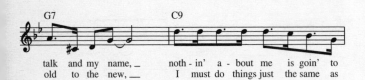

talk and my name, _ noth - in' a - bout me is goin' to
old to the new, ___ I must do things just the same as

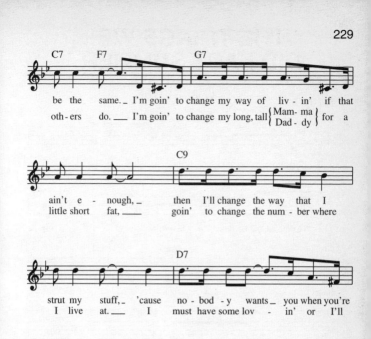

| C7 | F7 | G7 |

be the same._ I'm goin' to change my way of liv- in' if that
oth- ers do. __ I'm goin' to change my long, tall {Mam- ma / Dad - dy} for a

| C9 |

ain't e - nough, _ then I'll change the way that I
little short fat, ___ goin' to change the num - ber where

| D7 |

strut my stuff,_ 'cause no- bod - y wants_ you when you're
I live at.__ I must have some lov - in' or I'll

| G7 | C9 | F7 |

old and gray, _ there'll be some chang - es
fade a - way, _ there'll be some chang - es

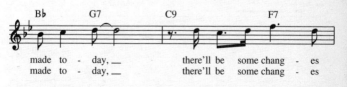

| Bb | G7 | C9 | F7 |

made to - day, _ there'll be some chang - es
made to - day, _ there'll be some chang - es

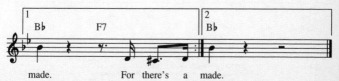

| 1 | | 2 |
| Bb | F7 | Bb |

made. For there's a made.

THE THINGS WE
DID LAST SUMMER

Words by SAMMY CAHN
Music by JULE STYNE

THIS YEAR'S KISSES

from the 20th Century Fox Motion Picture ON THE AVENUE

Words and Music by
IRVING BERLIN

Slowly

Cmaj7   Em7   A7

This   year's   crop   of   kiss - es

Dm7   G7   Dm7   G7

don't   seem   as   sweet ___   to

Cmaj7   Dm7   G7

me. ___

Cmaj7   Em7   A7

This   year's   crop   just   miss - es

Dm7   G7   Dm7   G7

what   kiss - es   used ___   to

Cmaj7   Gm7   C7

be. ___

Fmaj7

This   year's   new   ro - mance ___

TUXEDO JUNCTION

Words by BUDDY FEYNE
Music by ERSKINE HAWKINS,
WILLIAM JOHNSON and JULIAN DASH

THE VERY THOUGHT OF YOU

Words and Music by
RAY NOBLE

The ver-y thought of you, _____ and I for-get to do _____ the lit-tle or-din-ar-y things that ev-'ry-one ought to do. _____ I'm liv-ing in a kind of day-dream, I'm hap-py as a king, and fool-ish though it may seem, to

WHAT A DIFF'RENCE A DAY MADE

English Words by STANLEY ADAMS
Music and Spanish Words by MARIA GREVER

WHAT ARE YOU DOING NEW YEAR'S EVE?

By FRANK LOESSER

Slowly and sentimentally

May-be it's much too ear-ly in the game,_
Won-der whose arms will hold you good and tight,_

ah, but I thought I'd ask you just the same,_
when it's ex-act-ly twelve o'-clock that night,_

what are you do-ing New Year's,
wel-com-ing in the new year,

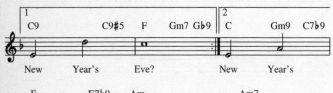

New Year's Eve? New Year's

Eve. May-be I'm cra-zy

to sup-pose I'd ev-er be the

one   you   chose.   Out of the thou - sand

in - vi - ta - tions   you'll   re -

ceive.   Ah, but in case   I

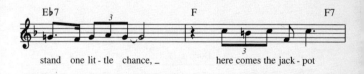

stand one lit - tle chance, _   here comes the jack - pot

ques - tion in ad - vance, _   what are you do - ing

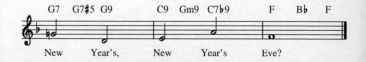

New   Year's,   New   Year's   Eve?

WHAT'S NEW

Words by JOHNNY BURKE
Music by BOB HAGGART

WEEP FOR ME

Words and Music by
ANN RONELL

Wil - low weep for me, __ wil - low weep for me, __

bend your branch-es green __ a - long the stream __ that runs to sea. __

Lis - ten to my plea, lis - ten, wil-low, and weep for me. __

_____ Gone my lov - er's dream, __

love - ly sum-mer dream. __ Gone and left me here __ to weep my tears __

__ in - to the stream. __ Sad as I can be,

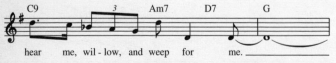

hear me, wil - low, and weep for me.

YOU TOOK ADVANTAGE OF ME

from PRESENT ARMS

Words by LORENZ HART
Music by RICHARD RODGERS

YOU TURNED THE
TABLES ON ME

Words by SIDNEY MITCHELL
Music by LOUIS ALTER

You turned the ta- bles on me, ___ and now I'm
fall- ing for you. ___ You turned the ta- bles on me, ___
I can't be- lieve that it's true. _____
I al- ways thought when you brought ___ the love- ly
pres- ents you bought, ___ why had- n't you brought ___ me more?
But now if you'd come ___ I'd wel- come
an- y- thing from ___ the five ___ and ten ___ cent store. ___

YOU'D BE SO NICE
TO COME HOME TO
from SOMETHING TO SHOUT ABOUT

Words and Music by
COLE PORTER

sire. _____ Un - der stars,

chilled _____ by the win - ter, _____

_____ un - der an Aug - ust moon,

burn - ing a - bove. _____ You'd be

so nice, you'd be par - a -

dise to come home to _____

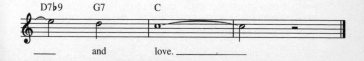

_____ and love. _____

GUITAR CHORD FRAMES

	C	Cm	C+	C6	Cm6

C

	C#	C#m	C#+	C#6	C#m6

C#/Db

	D	Dm	D+	D6	Dm6

D

	Eb	Ebm	Eb+	Eb6	Ebm6

Eb/D#

	E	Em	E+	E6	Em6

E

	F	Fm	F+	F6	Fm6

F

This guitar chord reference includes 120 commonly used chords. For a more complete guide to guitar chords, see "THE PAPERBACK CHORD BOOK" (HL00702009).

	C7	Cmaj7	Cm7	C7sus	Cdim7
C			3 fr		

	C#7	C#maj7	C#m7	C#7sus	C#dim7
C#/Db			4 fr		

	D7	Dmaj7	Dm7	D7sus	Ddim7
D					

	Eb7	Ebmaj7	Ebm7	Eb7sus	Ebdim7
Eb/D#		3 fr			

	E7	Emaj7	Em7	E7sus	Edim7
E					

	F7	Fmaj7	Fm7	F7sus	Fdim7
F					

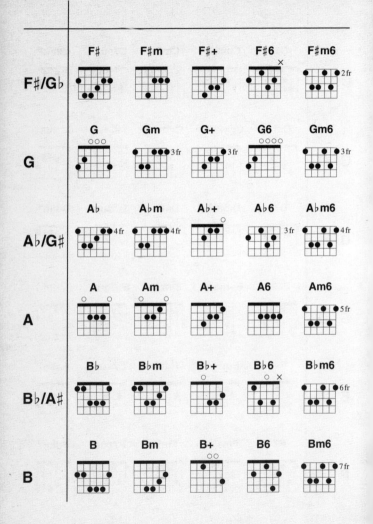

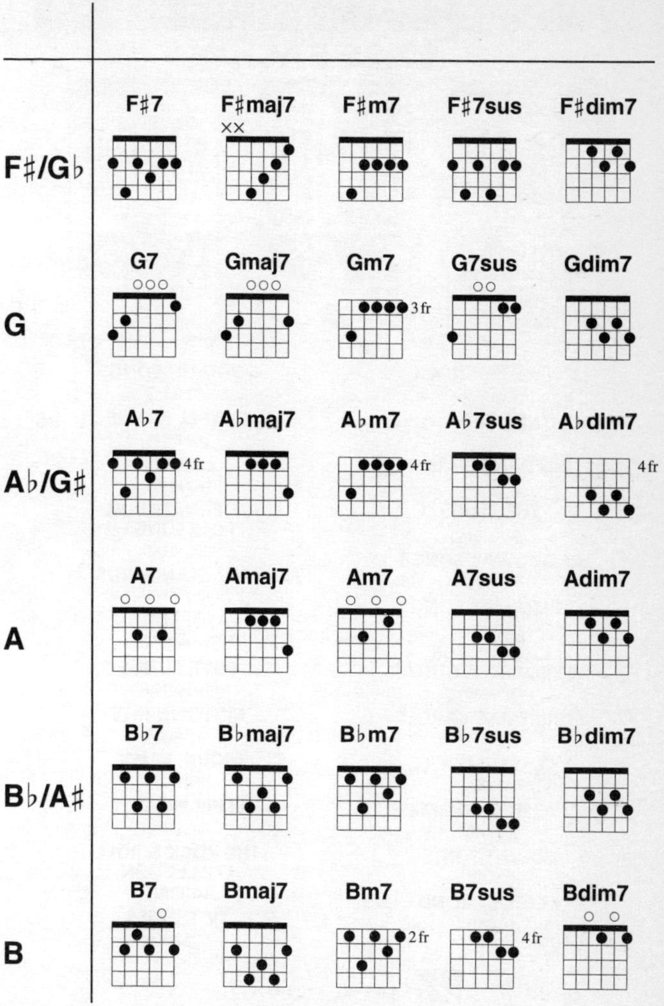
F♯/G♭
F♯7
F♯maj7
F♯m7
F♯7sus
F♯dim7
G
G7
Gmaj7
Gm7
3 fr
G7sus
Gdim7
A♭/G♯
A♭7
4 fr
A♭maj7
A♭m7
4 fr
A♭7sus
A♭dim7
4 fr
A
A7
Amaj7
Am7
A7sus
Adim7
B♭/A♯
B♭7
B♭maj7
B♭m7
B♭7sus
B♭dim7
B
B7
Bmaj7
Bm7
2 fr
B7sus
4 fr
Bdim7

THE PAPERBACK SONGS SERIES

$7.95 EACH

'80s & '90s ROCK
00240126

THE BEATLES
00702008

BIG BAND SWING
00240171

THE BLUES
00702014

BROADWAY SONGS
00240157

CHILDREN'S SONGS
00240149

**CHORDS FOR
KEYBOARD & GUITAR**
00702009

CHRISTMAS CAROLS
00240142

CLASSIC ROCK
00310058

CLASSICAL THEMES
00240160

COUNTRY HITS
00702013

NEIL DIAMOND
00702012

GOOD OL' SONGS
00240159

GOSPEL SONGS
00240143

HYMNS
00240103

**INTERNATIONAL
FOLKSONGS**
00240104

JAZZ STANDARDS
00240114

LATIN SONGS
00240156

LOVE SONGS
00240150

MOTOWN HITS
00240125

MOVIE MUSIC
00240113

ELVIS PRESLEY
00240102

**THE ROCK & ROLL
COLLECTION**
00702020

TV THEMES
00240170

FOR MORE INFORMATION, SEE YOUR LOCAL MUSIC DEALER,
OR WRITE TO:

HAL•LEONARD®
CORPORATION

7777 W. BLUEMOUND RD. P.O. BOX 13819 MILWAUKEE, WI 53213

www.halleonard.com

0601